To Debra,

Thank you for
supporting this Project.

Leah Curtin
10/18/2000

Sunflowers in the Sand

STORIES FROM CHILDREN OF WAR

Sunflowers in the Sand

STORIES FROM CHILDREN OF WAR

text by Leah Curtin

illustrations by the children of Croatia

Madison Books

Designed and Produced by Ruder·Finn Inc.
Creative Director: Michael Schubert
Art Directors: Lisa Gabbay and Gail Garcia
Designer: Jessica Honikman
Editors: Sue Stovall and Dena Merriam

Printed and bound in Iceland by Oddi Printing Corp.

Library of Congress Cataloging-in-Publication Data

Curtin, Leah, 1942–

Sunflowers in the sand: stories from children of war/text by Leah Curtin; illustrations by children of Croatia.

p.   cm.

Includes bibliographical references.

ISBN 1-56833-141-X (cl. : alk. paper)

1. Yugoslav War, 1991 — Children — Croatia.   2. Children's drawings — Croatia. I. Title

DR1313.7.C56C87 1999

949.703 — dc21   99-32170
                                                         CIP

Contents

Acknowledgments

This book is dedicated to "the children of war" everywhere and especially to those who shared their stories in the innocent faith that anyone, anywhere would care to listen….

My special thanks to all the children who shared their stories with me during my four trips to Croatia and Bosnia. These trips were supported by The Franciscan Sisters of the Poor Foundation under a grant from the American International Health Alliance (AIHA). I want to thank Michael Hoffman, Executive Vice President of the foundation, who suggested that a book should be written as part of a fund raising effort, and David Valinsky, foundation National Vice President, for his efforts on behalf of the Croatian partnership. I also want to extend my warmest thanks to Sr. Joanne Schuster, President of the foundation, who traveled to Croatia to teach administrative teams at the hospitals in Zadar and Biogard how to create a foundation to underwrite care, and who asked me to write this book. Thank you Priya Chandra, AIHA's coordinator for Croatia, for arranging the meetings, facilitating the essential research and communication, and for your invaluable support. Many thanks and much appreciation to Maria Krocker-Tuskan, M.D., for her reviews of the manuscript, discussions of history and correction of errors. Many thanks also to Sue Stovall and Dena Merriam for their work in editing the manuscript and to Jessica Honikman for the beautiful work she did in designing this book. Needless to say that without Patricija Padelin, child psychologist at the hospital in Zadar, this book could never have been written. Thank you Patricija.

Preface

The most vulnerable victims of war are always the children. It is the children who suffer greatest the consequences of conflict, although they have no voice and play no part in events leading to war. With little understanding of history or religious and ethnic divisions, how can they comprehend the destruction and make sense of the inhumanity that suddenly engulfs their world?

It is tremendously disheartening to realize that we are as helpless today as at any time in the past to protect our young from the horrors of war, horrors that subject them to the worst of nightmares — rape, torture, dismemberment and brutal murder — forcing them to witness cruelties imposed on those they most love, mothers and fathers, sisters and brothers, grandparents and other relatives.

How are those children who survive to cope with what they have seen and how is it possible to imagine they will not remain within the circle of hate, someday seeking retribution for the atrocities visited upon themselves and their families?

The future of these wounded children is uncertain. Some will recover and build healthy lives. Others will not. While some choose to speak about their experiences, others choose to keep them locked away in their hearts hoping that over time the memories will subside. In the days following the war, the children of the Balkans received much assistance from relief organizations, psychologists, child therapists and religious organizations. Professionals working with these children encouraged them to express their feelings, since self-expression is considered the first step in the healing process. The children drew pictures; they told their stories. Their artwork gives visual imagery to their agony, their sadness and their hopes. It gives reality to accounts that many of us have only heard about and have had difficulty believing possible in our modern world. Their stories are powerful reminders of how much work remains for us to do if we are to ensure a safe world, a world of redemption for our children.

The experiences told by the children are not just the experiences of one community. Similar stories have been gathered from children on both sides of the conflict. Brutality is not reserved for one group alone, or indeed for one particular war. These accounts represent the stories of children everywhere who become the silent pawns of adult conflict. They show children struggling to survive and enduring many hardships in the effort to make it through one more day.

It is impossible to read these stories and not be filled with overwhelming remorse that any child should suffer these atrocities, that we adults have not yet found a way to spare them the fallout of events they took no part in creating. Our hope is that this book draws attention to the plight of children in all regions of the world now engaged in conflict. Continued violence will only bring more pain. It is our hope that by sharing the experiences of the children of the Balkans, readers will feel inspired and committed to work toward a world where children are free from suffering the indignities of war.

Tony Danza
June 1999

… the paintings are visual metaphors

that express the children's fears and hopes.

Introduction

"About 2000 children remained in the town [Vukovar]. These children, some with their parents, but frequently without them, spent 86 days underground in cellars and shelters, seeing neither sun nor the sky without the constant hail of missiles, bringing dust and life-threatening danger 9,000 times a day, falling around them. If they were to go up to their flats for a moment on a higher floor, they could be hit by a mortar. Several were killed in this way and many more were wounded."[1]

According to UNICEF, the ratio of soldiers to civilians wounded or killed in armed conflicts during the twentieth century has reversed itself. In World War I there was one civilian killed or wounded for every nine soldiers, while in today's conflicts, there are nine civilians to each soldier casualty.[2] About 60 percent of civilian casualties are children. As appalling as these statistics are, they do not reveal the reality the children endure. Stories do. This is a book of stories told by the most innocent victims of adult politics — the children.

My interest in the children of the Balkans came through my association with the Franciscan Sisters of the Poor, who were working with a hospital in Zadar, Croatia. I had known the sisters for many years and had been inspired by their dedication and courage. My own nursing background and experience in healthcare management had led to a long-term relationship with them as a speaker and consultant. So when Sister Joanne Schuster from the Franciscan Sisters of the Poor told me about their work in Eastern Europe and specifically Croatia, and approached me about visiting children at a hospital there for a book project, I could not resist. However, I was unprepared for the reality I encountered, the hardships experienced by these children, and all innocent victims of war.

Social workers and psychologists have described the children's traumas: loss of family members, especially one or both parents; loss of parental support and protection; loss of home and family living; malnutrition; incarceration, sometimes in detention camps but usually in attempts to keep them from harm; loss of personal space; loss of physical abilities if the child was wounded; loss of a sense of security and stability; loss of innocence (a naïve belief that others will not harm you); loss of educational opportunities and school life; problems associated with living in an extremely poor environment with stressed adults — exposure to horrors that no one, certainly not children, should ever have to endure.[3]

How do the children themselves perceive these experiences? In this book, I use both the visual expression of the experiences of the children of the Balkan conflict and their own words to tell the world what it is like to be a child caught up in the incomprehensible world of adult hatred and conflict. When their stories have been told, it usually has been in journals, in articles written by and for professional caregivers. This book is a compilation of stories told from the children's point of view. I have attempted to hear what they have to say, and relate it as accurately as I could. The children's stories and recollections were gathered in interviews with them and their families, in dialogue with professional colleagues, and through review of the relevant literature.

The children's art contained in this book was collected by Patricija Padelin, child psychologist at the hospital in Zadar, and some of her colleagues: By Suncokret, a voluntary Croatian refugee organization located in Zagreb, and during my four trips to Croatia and Bosnia. Some were drawn during and after the war, and some were drawn during my interviews with the children to help them express their experiences. The children were asked to paint pictures not of what they saw but of what they felt. They were also encouraged to depict scenes from their lives before the war. Most of the paintings are visual metaphors that express the children's fears and hopes.

To protect the children's identities, their names have been changed. Some of the stories are amalgamations of their experiences and some are extrapolations. Nevertheless, they are accurate descriptions of what the children endured, experiences told by them for the rest of the world to hear.

1. Bosnac, V. "The Suffering of Children in Vukovar," *Archives for Mother and Child Health*, vol. 36, no. 2–3, p. 105.

2. Zivcic, Ivanka. "Emotional Reactions of Children to War Stress in Croatia," *Journal of the American Academy of Child & Adolescent Psychiatry*, vol. 32, no. 4, July 1993, p. 709.

3. Ajdukovic, Marina and Dean. "Psychological Well-Being of Refugee Children," *Child Abuse & Neglect*, vol. 17, pp. 844–845.

Everything that has happened

to each child matters.

chapter one

Patricija Introduces the Children

Patricija didn't trust me at first. "People want to come and see these children, especially the ones who were wounded. We're supposed to display them for a few *kuna* to journalists from Germany, England, France, the U.S. — as if they were freaks in a carnival. So, you get a story — the people who read it can thank their God that they have been spared. And it doesn't matter that you've hurt the children all over again...." But it *does* matter. Everything that has happened to each child matters. It matters to God. It should matter to the whole world, and certainly it matters to me. When Patricija began introducing me to the children, the need *not* to exploit, the need to be true to the task at hand, weighed heavily on my conscience.

I'd met a remarkable woman, Patricija Padelin, a child psychologist who worked with the children of Zadar, Croatia before, during, and after the war. She understands their problems and she walks through their fears with them, because she shared them herself.

"I was scared like a rabbit," she said. "I shook with fear."

"But you didn't leave, and you could have, couldn't you?" I asked.

"Oh, yes ... my grandfather has a home on the island of Korcula. I could have gone there." She said, "In fact, I did once for a few weeks. I took the ferry, the Jadrolinija. I did not know then that it was full of ammunition that was being smuggled around Croatia, which is probably a good thing because I would have died of fear just to think that if a shell hit the boat, we would all explode! There was only one other passenger, an Italian "journalist" who drank himself through the nightlong trip. Korcula was beautiful and safe, and everyone there has known me since I was a child. But I had to come back...."

I think Patricija is the bravest person I've ever met. But then, I have met some very brave young people — like Darija and Neven.

Darija, now thirteen years old and living just outside the town of Biograd, told me, "War is nothing like I thought it would be. Not like on television, not like in books, not like anything you could even begin to imagine. Tell the children of America that I hope for them, they never learn what war is. It is to be so afraid that you cannot sleep even when there are no bombs. It is to see everything, *everything*, destroyed. I cannot speak of those who are dead … my heart is still in bandages. I am happy I am still alive, but I am ashamed, too."

Darija's parents sent her to stay with relatives in the Czech Republic when it became clear that the war would last indefinitely. Neven, who at 19 speaks seven languages, was my translator on two of my four visits. Neven spent most of the war in Zadar and the rest as a refugee in Rome. He stoically translated Darija's words — later he added some of his own. He told me tales of the bombings and of collecting shells (only *some* of them spent) in the streets around his home. Of hauling drinking water from trucks, protecting churches and historic buildings with sandbags — and of sewer systems that no longer work. I will tell you the stories of children like Neven and Darija, for theirs is the *lived* experience of war as seen from the eyes of a child. And in that experience we may find hope for a future of peace.

I believe that you cannot understand a people unless you understand their history and culture. For this reason, I always visit museums when I am traveling. I try to learn about the people through their history. You can also learn a great deal about people if you can explore their myths and religions. And the stories they tell their children….

Once upon a time there was a hedgehog, a very special fellow named Ježa, who loved his home under a rotting log in the forest simply because it was his home — no amount of badgering or ridicule could lessen his love for home.

This Croatian folktale is a metaphor of a people's love for their homeland — no matter what others think, no matter the discomforts and dangers, in peace and in war, home is home. This is true for children, too, and for all their life long, I thought, as I returned home from my first trip to Zadar.

I rounded the cut in the hill to see my city, my home, sparkling with lights in the dusk. I tried to imagine how I would feel if 3,000 bombs and missiles fell here each day — on my home — for over three years. That is precisely what happened in Zadar. Swallowing the lump in my throat (I had no idea that I'd care that much!), I began thinking of another child, Amira. How could anyone exploit little seven-year-old Amira, who, with big, solemn brown dry eyes, said, "They kill my house … they kill my mama … they even kill my cat!"

All was silent when a

grenade hit the cellar....

chapter two | Amira Hides in the Cellar

`Amira, her sister Lejla, her brother Jusuf, her mother, and her grandmother — along with neighbors, about fourteen people in all — sought shelter in their basement during the attacks on Skabieja. Amira and Lejla, and the others, were very quiet as soldiers searched the streets. For three days and three nights, they hid. It was hot and stuffy, the smells worsening as the hours passed, but there was plenty of food and wine, for Mama stored their reserves in the cellar. Mama held Amira much of the time and Amira held her cat, Pepa. Grandmother told them stories to pass the time … it was very dark. Amira slept on the floor, her head in Grandmother's lap, alongside her sister and Pepa. Sometimes the adults lit a candle and played cards, but all went black when they heard gunshots or voices or footsteps. On the evening of the third day, the only two men in the group, Danijel and his son, Mile, decided to see whether or not it was safe to leave. No one had heard anything or anyone outside in the street for many hours. Perhaps it was safe….

Jusuf wanted to go with them, but Mile told him that someone had to stay and protect the women. Jusuf, who was twelve, was not sure they were being honest with him — but it was true that someone had to stay. Mama doused their little candle. Grandmother took Amira in her arms and turned toward the corner of the cellar, her back toward the opening, as Danijel and Mile slipped silently into the night. Jusuf stood by the door, watching. Moments later, Amira heard gunfire. No one said a word. No one even breathed. All was silent when a grenade hit the cellar…. Amira and Lejla survived. Mama and Grandmother and Jusuf and five other people died. And Amira's cat.

To this day, Amira dreams of parts of human bodies floating in wine — she wakes, calling "Mama," and shaking. Lejla, who is almost fourteen now, tries to comfort her, softly singing a lullaby, rocking her back and forth in her arms until Amira falls asleep again. Amira and Lejla now live in a children's home. When they are not in school, they sit near the square looking at the face of every man who passes by. They are searching for their father. Tata has been missing for several years, and Lejla is afraid that he might not recognize them anymore … but she *knows* she will recognize him. Amira cannot remember Tata at all; still, she helps Lejla look.

Lejla wants to be a schoolteacher when she grows up. "Amira, however, says she will own a pet shop — she will have ten cats, all named Pepa." When I look at the set of Amira's chin when she says this, I believe her.

My first trip to Croatia was limited to Zadar, but subsequent trips expanded my horizons considerably. Not only did I interact with children who had been wounded or psychologically scarred (and, many times, both), but also with children living in a variety of circumstances and places; all had important stories to tell. One of the first young men I met in the refugee camps in Zagreb was about twenty and very self-possessed. Davor does not consider himself a victim — he certainly does not want anyone to feel sorry for him. He doesn't live in the refugee camp, he works there! If asked, he will tell you that he takes care of himself. He does not want to speak of the war. He doesn't want to be seen as different from anyone else.

He has some bad memories, that's all. "I am *as* normal *as* anyone else," he declares. "It's the world that's crazy, not me. I will be fine if people like you would go away!" Perhaps. Perhaps not. There can be little doubt that Davor, and many thousands like him, are "normal" people caught in insane situations. He still feels responsible for his brother and sister and works and provides for them even though they now live with relatives.

Amira, however, says she will own a pet shop —

she will have ten cats, all named Pepa.

And he watched while the soldiers

booby-trapped the bodies and he was afraid.

chapter three

Davor Leads the Children

He who fights and runs away may live to fight another day … or may not, as the case may be, Davor thought. Davor, sixteen, and his younger brother Petar (seven) and sister Ana (ten) hid in the woods outside their village near the town of Slunj about 30 kilometers from Karlovac, which was about 50 kilometers from Zagreb. Heavy fighting in Slunj gave them advance warning — their parents urged them to move quickly — take nothing and run — they crossed the river to hide in the safety of the trees. Tata turned to Davor and said, "You're in charge here. Keep Ana and Petar quiet and hidden until we return. We must go back to find Grandma and get some food for the journey."

"Journey to where?" Petar asked.

"Hush," Tata said, "we'll be back as soon as we can and then we'll decide."

Tata was the youngest son in his family and so Grandma was his special responsibility. All of his brothers had left the village and the family farm to work in the city. Tata had remained to tend the farm and to care for Grandma — and when he married Mama, she moved into his family's home, which was where Davor, then Ana, and finally Petar were born. It was tradition. It had been so since anyone could remember.

As the war came closer, Mama begged Tata to leave — to go to Zagreb where his brother worked in a factory. *Where the family would be safe.* Grandma, however, would not leave her home. "I was married in this house. You and your brothers were born in this house. My husband died here. I will not leave it. Go, go without me. But I will remain here where I belong." Tata would not leave her alone — Mama would not leave Tata — so the family remained. However, Davor heard his parents talking and he knew that Tata was making plans to send them to stay with Uncle Mate in Zagreb.

Even with the sounds of shelling and gunfire close by — maybe even in the next village — Grandma refused to leave. So Mama and Tata took the children to safety, and then went back. She to get food and he to find Grandma before it was too late. Davor kept Petar and Ana quiet while they waited. When the sun was low in the sky, Davor decided to prepare a shelter for them. Petar was hungry and thirsty and he could not understand why Mama and Tata were taking so long. Davor didn't know either, but he did know the fighting was getting closer.

He kept Ana and Petar busy building and camouflaging a tree house. Petar stayed up in the tree while Ana and Davor scavenged for wood and branches filled with leaves. Davor was glad he had built many a blind when he and Tata and some of their friends had gone hunting; he was putting this knowledge to good use now. He settled Ana and Petar down in the blind and told them he would find something for them to eat *if* they stayed quiet. Then he climbed higher up in the tree. From his vantage point, he could see the flames clearly. The village was burning — but he did not tell his sister and brother. If they aren't here by morning, he thought, I'll take Ana and Petar to Uncle Mate's and come back to look for all three of them. When he climbed back down to the shelter, both Ana and Petar were asleep. A good thing, he thought, for he hadn't even looked for food.

The night was bad — shelling and bombing — automatic weapons firing. People nearby were screaming. Ana and Davor were awake for most of it, too afraid to move. Petar slept soundly as if he were in his own bed. When day dawned, Davor heard a soldier giving commands. Davor told Ana and Petar to be silent and he swiftly climbed to his "crow's nest" in the tree. He saw soldiers on the other side of the river building a barbed-wire corral with a wooden platform towering above it. It took the soldiers most of the morning to finish the work. Davor was not about to move his charges with enemy soldiers within earshot. So it happened that the three children were there, hiding in their tree house, when the enemy marched some prisoners into the corral and opened fire. The children were too far away to recognize faces, but Davor knew only too well who was being shot. He wanted to see if anyone was left alive. He wanted to know if his father and mother were among those gunned down by the soldiers … he had watched while the soldiers booby-trapped the bodies and he was afraid. And there was Ana and Petar. Suddenly, the silence was complete. Not even a bird called. The birds couldn't make sounds because they were gone — refugees from the shelling — and it would be years before they returned.

I've got to get the kids out of here soon, Davor thought. His chance came the evening of the massacre. He was hustling the children along, but Ana had to go to the bathroom, or wanted to rest, or her feet hurt her and Petar never ceased whining about food or asking about Mama and Tata. Davor knew better than to travel the roads, and the fields were mined. The safest way, he thought, would be to follow the river to Karlovac and try to find help there to get to Zagreb … and so it was that they followed the Korana.

At least they had water to drink … traveling by night, hiding by day. They met a neighbor, Goran Krizmanic. They asked if he knew what happened to Grandma and their parents. He didn't, but he offered to share some food with them and let them travel with him to Karlovac. From there, they made their way to Zagreb, where all was confusing and busy. But even strangers were kind to them, and Uncle Mate cried when he saw them, as he hugged each in turn over and over again. They were dirty and hungry — and their shoes were in tatters. But they were safe and Davor finally could sleep….

The children still live with their uncle and his family. Davor is a college student and Ana is entering high school, while Petar, who wants to be a jet pilot when he grows up, excels in math. Their parents are still missing, and presumed dead, but the children cannot mourn for them because they *must not stop hoping* that they are alive somewhere.

When we left the refugee camp, I asked Emil, who acted as my translator on this third trip to Croatia, what he thought. He said, "I think Davor is right. We are no different than any one else. I spent some of the war in Zadar, my hometown, and some as a refugee in Rome. But that is the only difference between me and your sons. Going to Rome is not an unusual thing to have happened, if you were a child living in Zadar at the time of the war. Many of the children from Zadar were sent to Rome for safety. You must ask Patricija when you return to Zadar; she helped make the arrangements."

"What was it like to be in Rome, Emil?" I asked.

"It was great!" he said. "We had fun … but we had worries, too. I was one of the older boys and eventually I was put in charge of the boys' dormitory — or at least I was in charge when no one else was there."

He saw soldiers on the other side of the river

building a barbed-wire corral

with a wooden platform towering above it.

… he lived with a group of other kids

whose parents had sent them away, too … to be safe.

chapter four   ✳   Emil Dreams of Home

He changed the rules, and even under the old restrictions, he won. Emil had to think that over. He'd been sitting on the door stoop playing "Solitare" for hours and lost every hand. Now he had won, and the only thing different was the rules he had changed in his head. Wow! he thought, I wonder if I could change all the rules in the world just by thinking about them. It'd be like having a magic wand in my head. Maybe I could even change the "rule" that put me here. He hadn't wanted to go, but when Tata spoke, that was that. And Tata said all the children had to go. Emil was sent away on a big bus full of children, and Mama and Tata stayed behind because they both worked in the hospital, and they were needed for the war effort.

Not that "here" was a bad place. "Here" was Rome. And now it was Spring. But "here" also was an apartment complex where he lived with a group of other kids whose parents had sent them away, too … to be safe. It was fun sometimes. In fact, a lot of times. Not to mention the fact that Marija was here in Rome. And Marija was the most beautiful girl in the world, even if he couldn't see her very often. The girls had to live in another building.

No parents, but still a lot of rules. The worst of two worlds, he thought. Maybe I ought to start "thinking" about some of those rules. Wouldn't it be great if I could change them? He almost laughed out loud when he thought of what his father might say about such changes. But Tata isn't here and I don't even know if he's still alive. Enough of that. Of course he's alive! I wish they had allowed Vuka to come with me. Why are there rules against dogs?

He looked over his shoulder. No one was looking, so he slipped the snapshots out of his backpack. He studied them closely. First he looked at the one of Vuka. Vuka was a real dog. Big — not some stupid little fluff ball — strong, and fast. And Vuka loved him; no one would be able to hurt him with Vuka around. He put Vuka's picture on the back of the stack and looked at the one of Mama's smiling face — for maybe the millionth time. But no matter how hard he stared, he could not see the color of her eyes. Were they brown or maybe hazel? Surely they were dark. Tata's eyes were blue, he remembered that — and Vuka's were brown, of course. He'd been gone two years: He was only twelve when he left, and now he was fourteen — actually fifteen if you rounded it off. He looked a lot different now. Older. Bigger. He was even trying to grow a mustache. He wasn't sure that his parents would recognize him when they saw him again ... maybe he'd better shave off the mustache. He could always grow one again if he wanted.

Some kids walked by — locals. One guy looked down at him and said, "Why don't those people go someplace else?"

A girl laughed mockingly, and said "You'd think they'd at least get out of our way!"

"You want me to make him?" the boy asked.

"Don't bother," she answered.

Emil got up and walked inside — slowly, so they wouldn't think he was running away from them. They can go to hell, he thought. Do they think I'm so dumb I don't know Italian? Or maybe they don't care. Do they think I want to be here? Who needs them? I hate them. I hate being here. I just want to go home! They'll be sorry someday. He threw himself down on his bunk. He'd gotten stuck with the lower bunk because Dean got there first and claimed the top one. All I've got is a bunk and a backpack, he thought. I can't even have the bunk I want. It figures.

He pressed his face into the pillow and gritted his teeth; he would go home. And his parents would be there. And Vuka would be so happy to see him that she would race around the outside of the house and roll in the grass and wag her tale so fast that her whole butt would move. And all my friends

… *Vuka loved him; no one would be able*

to hurt him with Vuka around.

will be there, he thought, except Viktor, who was killed in the shelling before I left for Rome. And I will never come back to Rome again — or, if I do, they'll wish they'd been nicer to me! Slowly his thoughts turned to how bad they'd feel when he came back rich and famous. And maybe he'd save that girl — the one who laughed at him — from a fate worse than death. As his anger receded, he daydreamed his way into a deep sleep.

Soon he was dreaming. He was back in Zadar, in the square facing the Cathedral of St. Stosija. It was noon, and the sun glistened on the white marble cobbles, but no one was around — and the sirens were deafening. He felt disoriented and even a little sick. The church, its entire facade covered by scaffolding filled with sandbags, looked like a bizarre brown turtle squatting where an ancient cathedral ought to be. But he knew it was the church. A woman dressed in an old housecoat and a kerchief scuttled quickly along one side of the square, keeping close to the storefronts as she rushed for shelter. "Run, run!" she shouted. And then the bombs were falling. Shrapnel. Dust. Greasy black smoke. The smell of cordite. Emil dove into a side street and rolled into a deep doorway. He crammed his head into the corner of the doorway and put his arms over his head.

He felt a thin, burning sensation across the calf of his leg, and then something fell on his back. It didn't hurt much, but the dust was so thick he couldn't breathe, so he pulled his shirt over his mouth. The noise was deafening. It lasted a long, long time but, Emil did not move. He was nauseated and sweating and terribly thirsty, but he didn't move an inch. And then it was quiet — very, very quiet. After it was quiet for a long time, he scrambled out from under the debris. His leg hurt badly, worse than anything he'd ever felt before, but he could use it.

He saw the woman who tried to warn him — at least he thought it was she — and she was dead. Across the square, over near the cathedral, he saw one of the big stone balls that used to be on top of the gatepost, rolling on the ground. He tried to lift it, but it was far too heavy. A man he'd never seen before lifted the sphere and took it inside the sandbags, carefully laying it beside other damaged bits and pieces of building and statues and clay roof tiles. "Mother of God," Emil heard the man whisper, "they will not destroy our church!" Emil knew as long as the man was praying, they could not....

And then everyone was everywhere, trying to find loved ones, looking to see what was left, helping to clear debris. All working together, moving with a purpose, rushing by Emil as if he weren't even there … and his leg hurt. He tried to ask for help, but the words were stuck in his throat — and there was so much noise. Emil felt utterly alone … and he thought he would die. But still no one noticed. Then a big man wearing a World War II field soldier's helmet scooped him up and yelled for the medics. The next thing Emil remembered was his mother calling his name and crying … and his father swearing that both Marko and Emil were going to Rome now!

Emil awoke with a start. His bed was soaked with sweat. He got up and checked the time. It was 2:00 a.m. and quiet, except for some kid snoring and another one crying — from the smell, he thought Marko had wet his bed again. Slowly, Emil sat back down, took off his leg, and massaged the stump.

The doctors in Rome had fitted him with an artificial limb — now no one can tell he has only one leg unless he rolls up his pants leg, which he won't do for anyone voluntarily. I did not know that Emil had an artificial limb until I heard his story — only some of which came from Emil. His mother, who is a nurse, told me the rest. When the hostilities ceased, Emil and Marko returned home to Zadar, where they live with their parents. Vuka did not survive the war, having died in the shelling. In fact, many pets were killed or were left to fend for themselves. Both Emil and Marko are now university students and both are doing well. Or, at any rate, Marko is doing well, and Emil is doing as well as could be expected, considering that Marija just broke up with him. He still has nightmares, but he doesn't talk about them anymore. Lucky for me that Emil needs to earn extra money; he is my ears and my mouth while I am in the refugee camps.

When I returned to Zadar, Patricija and Danijel met me at the airport — or what's left of it. It was a strategic target for the bombers during the war and repairs are still being done. On the way into town, I asked Patricija about the refugee children from Zadar. "The situation was very bad and the parents wanted the children sent to safety. It was dangerous, too. Imagine, if you can, having to decide who among the children would be sent on the next boat. And imagine, if you can, that one child is sent and another must wait and the child who had to wait is injured in a raid. And think what the parents might do to the one who made that decision. I thank God I was not the one to decide; one of our physicians, a psychiatrist, made those decisions. I only helped with the children — helping them say goodbye to their parents, getting them organized and on board the boats and buses. Some of the children left behind were maimed in the shelling. I remember one man who muscled his way into my office and slammed his fist on my desk. 'You would not send Drago — now we may lose him.' I was afraid he would attack me, but one of the doctors heard him and came in to help. 'Do not holler at her,' he said. 'I am the one who makes these decisions. Come, let us talk about it.' 'What is there to talk about?' Drago's father asked and he was still very angry, only now not with me. Many times, however, I could not sleep for worrying about the children who could not go and many were the nights I lost sleep because I worried about the children who did go."

"There were risks, yes," said Danijel. "You ask Patricija. She knows a boy, Dragi, who stayed and helped his father run guns. Perhaps she will tell you."

And then the bombs were falling.

Schrapnel. Dust. Greasy black smoke.

"It was on this trip

that something terrible happened…"

chapter five ✳ The Story of Dragi the Gunrunner

When I asked Patricija about Dragi and gunrunning, she said, "Language is such a problem. What is to tell about Dragi? First, let me show you." With that, she took me to the main administration building and down to the basement. She turned on the lights and pointed to one area and said, "That was the operating room, and over there was X-ray, and here was where we lived. At first many of us stayed in our own homes, but it became very dangerous to try to get in to work, so soon we all lived here in the basement where we worked. It was strange, but soon we became accustomed to it." She stopped and thought a minute. "It is amazing how adaptable the human animal is … soon it was as if we had always lived and worked in this basement. After Skabrnja, where 180 villagers were massacred, things became very tense. People were very afraid."

Patricija stopped speaking and took me to another section of the basement. "Here is where we had our intensive care unit," she said. Three-tier bunk beds were still in place. I tried to picture desperately wounded patients in them, and what it must have been like to care for people in bunks! As I looked around, I saw some pictures still taped to the wall, and over them was a sign, "House of Pain" (written in English). I asked Patricija about the pictures and she said that some of the children, who were patients here during the war, drew them. "But," she said, "I thought you wanted to know about Dragi. It is here that I met him. He was brought in with severe burns, and he still has many bad scars that cause him much pain, only now it is psychological pain. I will ask his father if you may interview him. Dragi's father and mother separated long before the war began, and Dragi lived with his father, who is a truck driver. Often Dragi would accompany his father on his trips when school did not interfere.

During the war, of course, there was no school and it was difficult to find a place that was safe for Dragi … so Dragi became the right-hand man of his father. But he will tell you more, if it is to be."

Some days later I met Dragi's father, who wanted to know why I was there and what I was about and what I wanted with Dragi. After talking with me, he promised that he would tell Dragi and it would be up to him if he would talk to me — Dragi, after all, was a man of fourteen now. One universal characteristic of human nature is curiosity — Dragi was curious enough to want to meet me and, after a while, to talk with me a little.

Dragi told me that he loved to travel with his father and at first he thought the war was very exciting. Most of the other children had to hide in cellars or were sent away, but he was part of the war effort. In a way, a soldier! Dragi's father drove the water trucks that brought water to the people of Zadar and Biograd, Sibenic and other towns where people would have nothing to drink, if it were not for them. This was dangerous work, and Dragi loved it, and would help people collect their water. He was not afraid of the guns and bombs — Tata drove well and fast and he knew many ways to get from here to there. Sometimes at night they would drive north, even beyond Zagreb, though he was not sure where. Only, at those times, Tata drove a car, usually and they would pick up loads of ammunition. Once they took someone's truck and picked up cases of guns and ordnance. I will let Dragi pick up the story from here.

"It was on this trip that something terrible happened. Even though it was night and we were not near any cities, someone started shooting at us — rockets! Tata pulled off the road and hid the truck. We camouflaged it as best we could and then we ran into the woods to hide. We heard enemy troops moving and talking. Then all was silent. We knew they were out there. We could feel it, smell it — but we did not know where, or whether they knew where we were. It was not hot, but I was sweating. And I knew that I was trembling. I had a tic in my right eye. I did not know how my father felt and I could not ask. We stayed where we were, rigid, hardly breathing — you cannot know what it was like — I do not know how long. A long time.

"It was about 4:30 when Tata touched my shoulder and indicated that we could move. Very slowly, very carefully, we moved back in the direction of the truck. We climbed in through the windows to be sure we made no noise. Then Tata started the truck and we drove like hell down the road. I was on the floor and my father drove with his head low, sometimes not even above the dashboard. Someone started shooting at us — I heard automatic weapon fire — but we kept moving. We were driving fast. It was bumpy and I was thrown around the floor. The next thing I knew I was in the hospital. My father said that the truck was hit and that it exploded. He managed to grab me and throw us both out of the cab before the explosion. We were splashed with gasoline and burned — as you can plainly see. My father was not hurt so badly as I was and his scars do not show like mine do. I have told this story many times to journalists from France and Germany, Italy, and even England. They all say it will be printed. If it has been, I have never seen it. You will be the same. Do you want to take pictures of my scars? Don't even think of it."

Patricija, who rarely left me alone with any child I was interviewing, intervened. "Dragi," she said, "thank you for helping with this project." She spoke in Croatian, which I do not understand. When Dragi got up to leave, I tried to express my gratitude. We both said "*Bog!*"[1] at the same time, and he smiled.

… as she rocked the baby Hrvoje to sleep …

someone threw a live grenade through the window.

chapter six

Hrvoje the Soldier's Son

Sergeant Ivan Pregrad had been concerned about his family's safety. They lived in a small village very near the front. And, of course, because he was a soldier, he was away from home much of the time. So he sent his family to live with his mother in Vukovar. As it turned out, Vukovar was one of the cities that ended up under siege — for three months the bombs and mortars fell, and then there was the invasion. Vesta Pregrad was a brave woman who protected her own and believed deeply in the goodness of God. In fact, she was praying her rosary as she rocked baby Hrvoje to sleep … without warning … someone threw a live grenade through the window. She shielded Hrvoje's body with her own just as it exploded and she was killed outright. The blast threw Hrvoje against the wall. He was buried in debris, where his older brother, Jure, found him. The children's mother, Rita, determined to save her baby, left Jure with a neighbor while she carried Hrvoje through the rubble-filled streets. Hiding from snipers and careful to avoid land mines, she made her way to the hospital — which was crowded with wounded people and those desperate to get help for them. Nonetheless, they urged Rita ahead of them because the baby was very badly injured and because "an injured child must be cared for first." He was rushed to surgery, and Hrvoje was saved … but not easily. He had a large blood clot on his brain and the doctors had to remove a piece of his skull to relieve the pressure. His eyes were injured. Shrapnel had severed the optic nerve in his right eye and lacerated the cornea in the left eye. Today, Hrvoje has a traumatic cataract in his left eye.

When I met Hrvoje, he was wearing a baseball cap and tossing a ball with his father in a parking lot. Hrvoje explained that he had to be careful because he had a "soft head." Otherwise, he assured me, he would play football, which "is a much better game." About one-third of Hrvoje's skull is still missing because there is no material available to replace it. As we climbed the stairs to the Pregrad's apartment, I learned that he really liked his teacher, his parents were going to take him to church tomorrow, and that he wanted to be a jet pilot when he grew up. His older brother, Jure, on the other hand, was reserved and very quiet — or, at any rate, he was when I was around.

"Hrvoje was only a baby when he was hurt," Jure informed me. Then he went into the kitchen with his mother. Hrvoje talked about school, about his Tata being a soldier, and on and on. Then both boys drew pictures for me while the grown-ups talked.

Ivan and Rita offered tea and cookies, and we talked about the war, and the economy, and what happened to Hrvoje. Just as I was about to leave, Ivan said, "I am a soldier. I went to war to protect my family and free my country. I knew I could be shot or killed. It was a risk I took," he hesitated for a moment. "But it is my mother who was killed and my baby son who was maimed." He hesitated once again and then plunged on. "I have these papers about Hrvoje, his medical papers. Would you read them and see if a doctor in United States could help him. I will pay whatever it takes."

The translator tried his best to tell me what the papers said. I promised that I would take the papers home with me and ask a physician to review them. When I returned, I gave the papers to a Croatian-American physician who shared them with colleagues. They believe that Hrvoje can be helped. Certainly a plate can be put in to protect the child's vulnerable (and very active!) brain. Although a personal examination is needed in order to be sure, the doctors also believe the traumatic cataract in Hrvoje's left eye can be successfully treated … a physician at the ophthalmology clinic in Oslo, Norway, offered to care for Hrvoje without charge. Hrvoje probably will not grow up to be a jet pilot, he *can* grow up to be almost anything else!

Hrvoje probably will not grow up to be a jet pilot,

he can grow up to be almost anything else!

She wants to forget there was ever a war,

but she cannot.

chapter seven ✳ ## Kristina's Problem

Today I met Kristina. She is sixteen years old and she has a problem. She wants to forget there ever was a war, but she cannot. Most nights she dreams about Zemunik, a village a few kilometers northeast of Zadar. And most nights she wets her bed. "Aunt Valentina says I must not tell anyone about this problem. She thinks that if I try hard enough, it will go away. She sets an alarm to wake me every two hours so that I can go to the bathroom, but still I have this problem. Aunt Valentina thinks it would go away if I stopped thinking about the war. And I swear that, except when I come here to talk, I do not think about the war — at least not when I am awake," Kristina assured me.

I also met Aunt Valentina, who seems very kind. She tries to be patient with Kristina's "problem," but it is very difficult for her. Valentina has two children of her own and her husband, Vlatko, had three children by his first wife, and now they have Kristina, too. "She is sixteen years old — far too old to be wetting her bed!" she said, and then she sighed. "She is my sister's daughter and I love her. My sister died in the war. She did not die from wounds or shelling. She had diabetes and there was no medicine for her, and so she died. She was married to a man who was a sergeant in the army of the former Yugoslavia. He made war against us. He helped shell Zemunik. I think he aimed the guns right at their flat. I do not know what has become of him and I do not care.

"We do not speak his name in our house. But Kristina knows. I worry about her. She has bad seed in her, but she is, after all, my sister's daughter and she will have a home with me until she marries. That is what I tell my Vlatko." She paused for a breath and reassured me, "We never say anything to Kristina about her father. Nothing. But she knows — and I think some of the children in her school know too. But what can you do except go on? That is what I tell Kristina. But how," she asked, "can Kristina get on with her life? Marry a nice boy when she still wets her bed? What husband would put up with such a thing?"

Kristina could not have been more than ten or eleven when her world went to war. She does not want a boyfriend. She does not want children. And she definitely does not want to wet her bed anymore. She dreams of being a dancer in Hawaii, and hopes that perhaps someday she will even appear on *Hawaii Five 0*. I haven't the heart to tell her that the television program has been out of production for decades. Surely it doesn't matter.

"In the first years that I lived in Zadar," Kristina said, "many of the other kids hated me because of my father. The teacher did not allow them to hurt me at school, but every day on the way home they threw stones at me. Every day I had to fight. Sometimes I even had to schedule the fights. And sometimes a whole gang would pounce on me and beat me. My cousins would help me when they could, sometimes … that is why I want to go to Hawaii. I hate it here even though it is not as bad now. But in Hawaii I could make a good life for myself — and I would be famous. And then they would be sorry. "[2]

Patricija arranged for one of the nursing assistants to take me to her mother's home in the village of Skabrnja. As we traveled by car along narrow roads, I saw devastation all around. In the villages, there is often even now, four years later, barely one brick left upon another.

She dreams of being a dancer in Hawaii, …

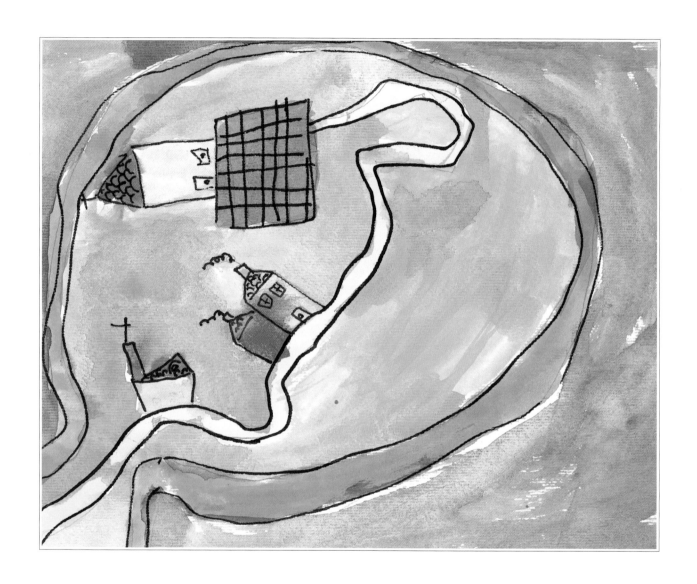

She was, in fact, rebuilding her own world.

chapter eight | # Grandmother Demands a Hearing

When we arrived in Skabrnja, we were greeted by a wonderful woman, Anamarija Klapan-Prenda — a grandmother who eagerly showed me the home she and her sons and her daughter and her daughters-in-law and her nephews and her neighbors were rebuilding with "a little help from the government."[3] Mrs. Klapan-Prenda is a short, stout, strong woman whose graying hair is covered with a babushka. The sleeves of her blouse are short, revealing well-muscled arms. She has a gap between her front teeth, sparkling blue eyes behind thick lenses — and enough energy to rebuild the world if necessary. She was, in fact, rebuilding her own world. She was living in the shell of a house, taking care of her animals, cooking over an open hearth — and depending upon friends and family to bring her water. She is wrinkled, tough, stubborn — a totally admirable woman!

She told me that when she was finally able to return to the village, only two things were left alive — the fish in her well (many villagers keep a certain kind of fish in their wells because the fish keeps the well "healthy") and four of her rose bushes that, although a bit scraggly, still bloomed. She seemed most outraged by what had been done to the village church, which she insisted that I see. "Can you believe that anyone would deliberately destroy God's own house?" she asked rhetorically. "Look. See. Even the sanctuary. There is nothing left. Nothing!" She stumped back to the house she is rebuilding to tell me her story. She offered us some fruit and cheese and some water her daughter had brought for her from the town. They have a well, and it is still intact, but they are afraid to use it because there is a bomb in the well along with her fish. She told me that there is no water in the village now — there won't be until she can use her well. And then we sat down to talk.

"I know," she said, "that you only want children's stories, but there is a boy in this story, so maybe you can tell it. Besides, I am a grandmother and I have some things to say!" I nodded and smiled — not that it mattered much. She was already launching, with great dignity and histrionic excellence, into her tale of terror. "I — Anamarija Klapan-Prenda — my youngest son and his wife and my three grandchildren lived together in our house in Skabrnja — the house of my husband's family, the house in which each of my three children were born. For many months the village had been under attack — bombing, shelling, sometimes someone would throw a grenade, nothing more," she began. "But my daughter-in-law was afraid, so she took the two youngest children and left for Germany, where she had some relatives. My son and his oldest son stayed here with me. One night while we were sleeping, the bombing started again — *very* close this time. The bombing was so heavy that Mihovil, my son, said that we must not even try to get to the bomb shelter in the church. Mate, my grandson who is fifteen, and I hid in the laundry area where there are no windows and Mihovil came with us, too. When it became quiet again, we went upstairs and back to sleep. We did not know that the bombing had stopped because enemy soldiers were invading our village. If we had known, we would have run away as any sensible person would have done!

"You may think it strange that we could go to sleep again, but the bombing and shelling had been going on for months. After a while, you learn to sleep when you can. Then, when I was finally sleeping soundly, someone shoved me out of bed with no warning. I hit the floor hard as I heard a soldier ordering me to lie face down. He was pointing a gun at my head. Then he ordered me to go to the church. 'Now!' he shouted. I grabbed my blanket to wrap around myself, and the soldier said, 'Leave it! Even the blankets belong to us now!' Another soldier who came from a nearby village — Nadin, I think — said, 'No, let the old grandmother have her blanket. What does it matter?' I did not know where Mihovil and Mate were, and I did not call out to them, for I was afraid the soldiers might kill them because they were men. I took my blanket and ran toward the church, the same one I showed you. On my way, I saw a house, one that had a basement, and I thought, this is a better place to hide … if they want me to go to the church, it is probably because they want prisoners. I ducked inside the basement to hide and found fifty or sixty other villagers hiding there. Mate was there, but not Mihovil. We stayed in that basement for a day and a half, and everyone was getting very hungry … so Mate ran back home when there seemed to be no one around and brought some food back. I would have gone myself, but I had no shoes. The beasts would not let me take my shoes with me, and as you might have noticed, there are many sharp stones." She stopped to take a drink of water and then continued. "Everyone in the cellar decided that we must plan our escape that very night before the soldiers came back. We did not know that they were still there! We planned to leave the cellar one or two at a time and make our way to the railroad tracks and then down to the coast — about 35 kilometers away — where we thought we could get help. It is very far, but what else could we do?

"When night fell, we started leaving the cellar as planned — only I did not head to the railroad tracks because I wanted to go home and get myself a pair of shoes. Naturally, I did not tell Mate because I wanted him to have a good chance to escape — not to be held back by an old grandmother. While I was in the house putting the shoes on my feet, I heard machine-gun fire and screams from the other side of the tracks — about 35 meters from my home. I was sure that the others were being shot. I ran from the house and headed in the opposite direction from the railroad tracks until I stumbled upon a woman who was crying over the body of her dead son. I tried to get her to come with me, but she would not leave him. It occurred to me that my daughter-in-law's grandmother might still be hiding in her house. This is not rational, but I thought, I must go to her house and help her if I could. It was pitch black and there was still sporadic gunfire and crying. But I found her house and entered. I could see nothing, so I struck a match — all of my daughter-in-law's family were dead. Her grandmother — ninety-six years old — had been stabbed seven times. The blood was fresh, so I knew the danger was near. I dropped the match and ran from the house. This time I ran toward the tracks because I thought they had finished their work there and would be gone — I wanted to find Mate if I could!

"I made it to the other side of the tracks and started looking everywhere for Mate, but he was no where to be found. Another woman, a very old woman, was looking for the body of her son. She could not find him either, but she did find the body of her grandson. Now the soldiers were coming back and they threatened to kill me. I asked them, I begged them, to let me take the old one to her home. 'You can go anywhere you want,' one of them said. 'You can go to Zadar. You can go to Biograd. But you will pay for it. This is an entirely different country now — you have no place in it!' So, very slowly, very carefully, I walked the old one back to her home. Later, I left her and started walking toward the Adriatic. Bodies were everywhere, but there was no time to stop and identify them. I prayed to the Virgin that Mate and Mihovil were not among them. I hid by day and traveled by night, and along the way, I met some others from my village. We were all hungry, very, very hungry — and looking for anything we could find to eat. I was looking everywhere and asking everyone about Mate and Mihovil — then someone told me they had seen Mate. He had been wounded and he was very sick. I asked where, and the man said about two kilometers back, near Galovac. So I went back. I found him but he was dead. He had died of a terrible fever from a wound in his leg."[4] She paused again for a moment and then said, "Do not ask me about this, for I have nothing whatever to say about it. I prayed for Mate, and some kind people, whom I did not know, helped me to bury him. It was not easy.

"This took two more days, but then I started walking toward the sea again. What else was there to do? Finally, I made it to the Adriatic and help. I was sent to Germany, where I spent some time with my daughter-in-law and her cousins. I told her about her family — and about Mate. I also had to tell her that I did not know what had happened to Mihovil. I stayed for a long while — several months. But it was very crowded and I had some cousins who had emigrated to Canada. I was able to get in contact with them and spent three and a half years in Canada. They were very kind, but home is home! As soon as I could, I returned to Croatia and to my village. I found what was left of my house and I kissed the walls, I was so happy to be home again. I did not know until I returned home, but Mihovil survived."

On the way back to Zadar, Patricija spoke to me of the courage of women like Anamarija Klapan-Prenda. Patricija also spoke of the hatred let loose in and by the war. "My grandfather was Serbian," she said, "and my grandmother, Croatian. I am torn in two by this war and so are many others like me. I do not know how we can heal this country, but I do know the worst threat to the children's future is not poverty or disease or wounds. It is *hatred*. Unless we can conquer it, there is no future."

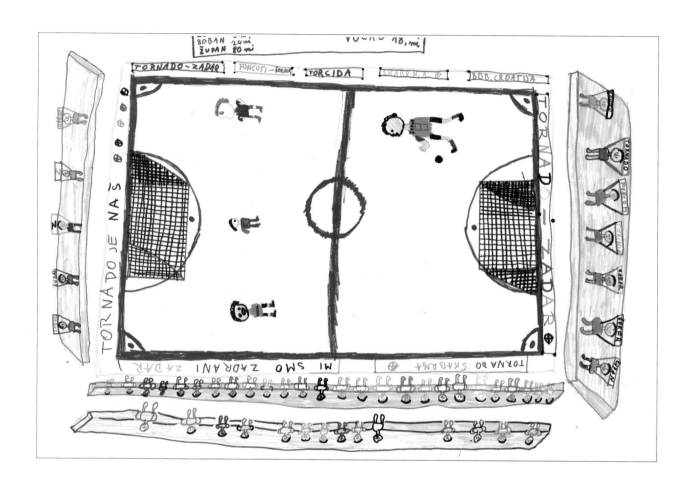

But they had survived … They were home once again …

chapter nine

The Children Return to Skabrnja

In August of 1998, I received a packet from Patricija. When I opened it, I was delighted to find 52 pictures drawn by the children of Skabrnja — and yet another story to tell. As work progressed in the rebuilding of homes, men risked their lives clearing fields so they could plant again (two men were killed by land mines while clearing their fields during the week before I visited Skabrnja). Anamarija Kaplan-Prenda's well was rescued from the bomb — she prevailed upon her eldest son, a police officer in Zadar, to appeal to his friends on the force to remove this terrible bomb from her well. They did so with no casualties, so there was once again water for the farmers in Skabrnja. Then the government rebuilt the schoolhouse — and all the townspeople worked to begin rebuilding their church. When all was ready, families returned to live in Skabrnja — the children came back.

So many of the children — Ivo and Edgar and Eduard and Mladen, Sara and Lucija and Ines and Kresimir, Frane and Alma and Karlo and Lovre — had been evacuees. So many children had lost parents and grandparents, brothers and sisters, cousins and aunts and uncles, friends and teachers. But they had survived. It was a great victory and a grand celebration. They were home once again — and their pictures reflect the joy. Moreover, Croatia was in the Olympics and the team was a serious contender for the World Cup in soccer.

Life began to settle into its comfortable routine. Fathers were harvesting crops or driving trucks and mothers were teaching school or working in the city. Each Sunday the people went to Mass and thanked God Almighty for peace and for their homes — and for one another. It wasn't perfect, but the problems were the sort of problems one expects to deal with in daily life. Under the serenity there was the sorrow, but it was bearable.

Patricija visited the village and talked with many of the children at the school. She asked them for the pictures — and for stories about themselves and what they will "be" when they grow up — the lady from America. I saw their pictures, and my heart lifted. Then I noticed a penciled note from Patricija. Written in haste on the piece of cardboard she'd inserted to protect the pictures from injury, it was barely legible. She wrote:

Dear Leah,

I have collected these pictures for you from the children recently returned to Skabrnja. But, since two weeks ago, when they drew them, three have been killed by land mines…

Patricija

As I read Patricija's note, I remembered her statement on our trip back to Zadar from Skabrnja. "The enemy," she had said, "was hatred. Hatred is what must be overcome if there is to be hope for the children." I believe her, but I do not underestimate the task. Especially when I think of the story about Matija — a young girl who lives in a camp near Zagreb.

"… Hatred must be overcome

if there is to be hope for the children."

… she could not draw anything.

She could only make splotches of paint.

chapter ten ❋ Rape of the Innocents

Some things hurt so much that the telling of them is too hard to do straight out. They need an introduction, if they must be told at all, in metaphorical terms. This, at any rate, is what I concluded when Matija told me her favorite story — the one about *The Fisherman Palunka*.

Once upon a time, there was a very poor fisherman who casts his net into the Adriatic and catches a most remarkable fish, a magical gold fish who promises the fisherman three wishes, if only he will let him go. "Let me go, and I promise you that you shall have your heart's desire for as long as I swim in the sea," the fish said. Palunka doesn't really believe that a fish can grant wishes, but he had never met a fish who talked before — so he decided to give it a try. "I wish that my family would be healthy and happy," he said, "and that my business will be prosperous." At that, he freed the fish, who swam happily away. Much to the fisherman's surprise, his wishes were granted. His business prospered and he and his family were very happy for many years. Then another man caught the magical gold fish — a man who did not believe the fish's promises. "Ho, ho," he said to the fish, "You are telling lies to cheat me of my dinner!" And with that, he killed the fish and ate him.

With the fish no longer swimming in the sea, Palunka's luck changed and soon he was poor again. I am poor, he thought, but at least I have a family who loves me. But then, one after another, his children sickened and died. And then his wife died. And now he was alone and sad, but not for long, because he drowns the next time he goes fishing. And that is the end of the story.

"Why do you *like* this story?" I asked Matija.

"Because," she answered, "I am like the fisherman, only smaller — I do not fish. I go to school."

"Is that all?" I asked.

"No," she said solemnly. "Now, do you want me to draw a picture or not?"

"Yes, I would very much like a picture. Will you draw me one of yourself for my memory book?" Slowly, over a period of several days, Matija told me pieces of her story — one of the workers in the refugee camp filled in the rest. This is Matija's story — or at any rate, as much of it as I can piece together.

Matija, who was six years old at the time, her baby brother, Roko, and her parents, Mirjam and Frane, lived in Krupac — a Bosnian village not far from Sarajevo. There were many bombs and mortars falling on Krupac, but Matija and her family were too poor to leave and perhaps Tata was too stubborn. Whatever the reason, they stayed at home while many of the other villagers fled. Miraculously, their little house was not too badly dam-aged, so they could still live in it. When the bombs fell, they would run to the bomb shelter for protection, but when all was quiet, they would return to their home. Month after month, their luck held, until one night, when all was quiet and Matija was sleeping soundly in her bed, soldiers came. Mama had only time enough to hide Matija in the woodpile, warning her to be very quiet — no matter what happened, she must not move or utter a sound. Mama had never spoken to her so harshly before.

And then the soldiers were there. They forced Tata to lie face down on the floor and pointed a gun at his head. One soldier took Roko, who was screaming. Another threw Mama on the floor. He hit her in the face again and again and he fell on top of her and hurt her "really bad." Then other soldiers came and did things to Mama, too. The soldiers, who had made Tata lie down on the floor, pulled his hair until his neck was bent and said many bad things to him as they slammed his face again and again into the floor. Then the soldiers shot both Mama and Tata in the head. The soldier who had Roko ripped his diaper off, slammed him against the wall and began bumping himself against Roko again and again.

When he was done, he threw Roko into a corner. At this, Matija cried out — and she was discovered. One of the soldiers grabbed her and took her into the bedroom and threw her on the bed and held her down. Then he hurt her terribly. He was still hurting her when someone yelled at him to come now — hurry! He ran away. Blood was everywhere. Matija tried to crawl to Mama. She could not walk. But Mama had no head anymore — and Tata did not move, no matter how many times she called to him. Roko was dead; she could see that. Matija vomited all over herself — that was how she was found, who knows how many hours or days later, dehydrated, delirious and covered with dried blood and filth.

She was taken to a hospital and then from one refugee camp to another until she ended up in Zagreb. She was withdrawn and frightened. A silent child who would not speak, rarely ate and never played. When she was given crayons or paint, she could not draw anything. She could only make splotches of paint. After years of help and gentle care, she is still very timid — she will talk if someone takes the time to listen. And she will draw pictures.

Matija was too much for me to bear. I needed to go home. I needed not to know any more. I told myself, who are you to say *you* can't bear any more. Nothing has happened to *you!* If Matija can live, and Emil and Amira and Davor, who are you to feel sorry for yourself? No more of this self-dramatization. Nonetheless, I did not sleep well that night. The next morning, there was more.

As I have mentioned earlier, many of the older citizens would not leave their homes and villages. And some of them, perhaps many of them, became victims of poorly disciplined, badly supervised troops. There is no reasonable explanation for "war crimes." There is no understanding them. And there is no way that it is possible to exact justice for them. It may be possible to *forgive* them, but in my darker moments, I cannot see how.

"We did not think the war would change anything,

certainly not for us. But we were wrong. …"

The Orphans' Horror Story

Ante and Luka and Doris lived in an orphanage near Vukovar. Ante is now twelve, Luka is fourteen and Doris is also twelve. They had always lived in this orphanage, as long as anyone could remember. Or at least that's what Luka said, and there is no doubt that Luka is the spokesperson for this little group. "When the war started, no one thought very much of it," Luka declared. (Luka does not merely speak, she *declares*.) "We did not think the war would change anything, certainly not for us. But we were wrong. When the bombing started, the teachers took us into the basement to hide. This went on for many days. When the orphanage was destroyed, we all ran away. Every place we looked was wrecked, but some offered places to hide and places to get out of the rain or snow. We had nothing left but each other and so we made a bloodpact. We would stay together no matter what — we would not let anything or anyone keep us apart. It is for this reason that we did not answer the calls of those who were searching for us, and it goes without saying that we tried our best to hide from the soldiers. We roamed the ruins by night, searching for food — we hid and slept during the day. When it was cold, we huddled together in a box made of debris — and lit a candle. You would be surprised how much warmth three bodies and a candle can make...."

"Sometimes we had to eat rats, which we caught with the traps we devised. It is a hard thing to believe, but there were many times when we were grateful for the boiled remains of rats. Sometimes we dreamed of catching one of the pigs that roamed the ruins looking for something to eat. One time we saw them — there must have been six or eight of them — eating the bodies of the dead. And we heard gunshots as someone killed them (the pigs that is) ... even the soldiers were repulsed by the pigs, and shot them. But always they took the carcasses away. The stench was awful. And we were too afraid to try to catch man-eating pigs anyway! So we stuck with the rats. We stole what we could, but there was never enough to eat, although we found plenty of things we could wear, except for shoes. But still we had each other.

"One night when we were very hungry, we got lost and when day broke, we had to hide in a strange place. It is very confusing when everything looks pretty much the same, which it often does in ruins — especially after dark. Be that as it may, we heard automatic-weapon fire and it was close by. We ducked and hid until we heard the voices of soldiers urging a ragged band of old people to 'move along.' Sometimes we heard the thunk and moan as one soldier or another hit one of them with the butt of his rifle. They took them to a church and some of the soldiers raped the old women, who screamed and fought with all their might. Believe me, I know about such things!

"But what happened next, I did not know about. The soldiers, some of them scratched and bleeding from the old women's claws, tied the grand-mothers to the pews. And the men, too. When they were secure, the soldiers started with the old lady who had made the most noise. They took out their knives and — it looked to me like they cut her face. She was fighting so hard that one of the soldiers had to hold her head while the other did the cutting. Then the soldier pulled something out of her face — and I knew what it was. It was her eye. Then they shoved her eye into her mouth and held her mouth closed and pinched her nose so she couldn't breathe. That meant, she had to swallow her own eye.

"I could not look anymore. I would not let Doris or Ante look either. We hid and kept very quiet. We tried to keep even from hearing, but we could not. They must have done this to each one of the old people — some of the soldiers laughed and said coarse words. All the while the old ones screamed and cried and begged for death. And then, when they were done with that, we heard the guns again. They murdered them. We did not move or even hardly breathe, not for a long time after they left. Not until daylight — which was a mistake. As we tried to make our way back to Vukovar, some townspeople saw us and chased us. I could have gotten away, but how could I abandon Doris and Ante? We were caught and eventually, we were sent to another orphanage. It was warmer and there was plenty of food. And they let us stay together. We do not speak of the time we were on our own or of what we did and what we saw. Unless someone asks. You asked."

"Such things no longer bother me — too much," Luka said. However, she did agree that she and Doris and Ante would draw pictures for me.

Despite my nightmares, the next day dawned and Patricija and Danijel agreed to take me on an excursion. "It is time," Danijel said, "for you to see a Bosnian town. We will go to Mostar." I was a little worried about trouble at the border, but Danijel said, "Do not be troubled. We will take the back roads through the mountains. There they usually are not so strict about who they let in … just keep silent and let me do the talking." The drive itself was memorable, the scenery being almost as breathtaking as the mountain curves taken at breakneck speed on a one-lane highway. True to his word, Danijel got us through the border check with a minimum of hassle — we were on our way to Mostar. "I have been wanting to get to Mostar to see what has been happening," Danijel said, rounding yet another bend and taking another ten years off my life.

As we entered the Croatian sector of Mostar, the fact that we were in a war zone became increasingly clear. Uniformed soldiers were everywhere — some held automatic weapons across their chests. We asked one of the soldiers guarding the new bridge for permission to enter the Muslim sector.

The old bridge, the pride of Mostar, a graceful arc spanning the Neretva River for over 700 years, was destroyed during the war. The soldier advised us not to stay too long because things were still tense. We walked across the new bridge and could clearly see the ruins of the old bridge down the river.

The utter devastation of Mostar was stunning. Pockmarks in ruined buildings gave mute testimony to the violence — there was not one square foot undamaged. Most of the roads had craters surrounded by the stereotypical marks of rockets and mortars and bombs. We were walking along a mostly stone and dirt road. It was evident that little had been done to repair the damage caused by war. School buildings, apartments and many shops were rubble. A few shops were open — most seemed to be jewelry stores — but often in buildings that had been only partially repaired.

However, many people were out — some sitting under colorful umbrellas in outdoor cafes, chatting and drinking Turkish coffee and soft drinks. No one bothered us. No one spoke to us. But we knew they were watching. As we approached the center of town, we passed the Iranian Embassy and then the Saudi Embassy — they were obviously open, flags flying. In the center of town, a park, upon closer inspection, looked more like a graveyard. Graves were everywhere, many of them very tiny graves. The years on the grave markers told the stories — 1991 – 1993 — on one near the temporary chicken wire fence that now surrounds the park-turned-graveyard. A mosque across from the park had been bombed out, although it was apparent that at least here, repairs were in progress. A sign told us that the rebuilding project is a gift of the Kingdom of Saudi Arabia.

Graves were everywhere,

many of them very tiny graves.

" … *This is our home, the home of our grandfathers,*

and their grandfathers before them … And we are staying."

chapter twelve ✳ The Home of My Grandfathers

While we were waiting for Danijel, an elderly man approached us and very courteously spoke to us. However, the dialect was so different that Patricija could not understand what he was saying. When Danijel returned, he took over the translation. The man wanted to know what we were doing there, so Danijel told him. When he understood the purpose of our visit, he started telling us what he thought must also be known — the stories of his people. "First you must understand why we remain here. It is because this is home. Everyone is always saying, 'Why don't you go home?' Why? Because this is home! My family has lived in Mostar for 700 years. If that is not home, what is home? If the problem is that we worship differently, it is no different than the way we have worshiped for all these centuries. Home is home! This is our home, the home of our grandfathers and their grandfathers before them. It is also the home of my grandsons. And we are staying."

"What of your grandchildren?" Danijel asked. "Dead. All dead," the man answered, sweeping his right arm in the direction of the park. "See for yourself the graves! Do we need to dig them up for you? All we have ever wanted is peace, not war! Now there is so much hatred. How can we find peace? You tell me!" Danijel said that all he wanted was peace, too — that only madmen wanted war.

"We have no need for 'ethnic cleansing' here," the man said. "What is to be 'cleansed'? Women? Children? Who?" Tears came to his eyes as he spoke. "Come, let me show you our town."

As he walked and talked, I wondered that he would even talk to us. Several times, he turned and said, "Please tell the people we want peace. My people do not want war, only peace. For our children and for yours." And then he would continue introducing us to shopkeepers and passersby.

I did not know until later that we were among the first non-military, non-Muslim visitors to cross the new bridge.

As we continued, I thought of Amira and some of the other families I had met in the refugee camps. What, indeed, needs to be "cleansed?" I wondered. The unspeakable horrors of war are themselves almost cleansed of their horror when analyzed and objectified — worse yet, when they are rhetorically justified, as happens when atrocity suits a particular military or political objective. There are no stories here, I thought sadly. Only graves.[5]

I was wrong, of course. There are as many stories as there are people, but often the stories are not what we thought they would be. *"There is a widespread notion that the most difficult thing for torture victims to speak about is the sexual abuse they have suffered. I think that this idea mostly originates in the minds and hearts of therapists. It is my experience from work with torture victims from many parts of the world that the most difficult thing to speak about is 'betrayal' — to have given information or betrayed comrades to the enemy."[6]* Such surely was the case for Josip....

" … My people do not want war, only peace.

For our children and for yours."

Josip ran home and hid in his room,

and after that day, things were not good for him.

chapter thirteen ✳ The Clean and the Unclean

Josip and his family lived in Mostar for many years. Josip's mother is Croatian and his father is a Muslim, but his father's father (Josip's grandfather) was Serbian. Before the war, Josip's family was very happy. When the war broke out, Josip's father joined the BiH Army, and his mother took Josip and his older sister to live with her parents in the Croatian sector of Mostar. Josip's mother's father had much to say about Serbs, and about the monsters in the BiH Army. Josip was confused and very sad. He loved his father, and he missed him, but he did not have the courage to say anything in Tata's defense. Josip felt guilty about this, especially when some of the children asked him about his father. "My father is a soldier," he would say, but he never told them in which army. Then one of the older girls said, "I know you. Your father is a Muslim *chetnik*!"

"No. No, he is not!" Josip shouted. But the girl laughed a mean laugh and started chanting, "*chetnik, chetnik, chetnik…,*" and pointing her finger at him. Josip ran home and hid in his room, and after that day, things were not good for him.

When word came of "ethnic cleansing", Grandfather arranged for Josip and his mother to go to Norway and live with some relatives. He was afraid for their safety. And so they went. And they *were* safe. But Tata was not. He was killed in the war. Mama found this out when they came back home after the war was over. Josip could not believe his ears when Mama told him that Tata was dead. He could not speak. He could not cry. All he could do was think, Tata is dead. I will never see him again. If only I had not let Grandfather say those things about him. If only I had … I cannot even tell him I am sorry….

When I talked to Josip, I asked him about his favorite story. He said it was "The Ugly Duckling." I asked him why — he said, "Because I am like the Ugly Duckling!"

"Are you, indeed?" I said. "Then you are going to grow up to be the most handsome swan of them all. Is this not so?"

Through his tears, Josip smiled and said, "Yes, that is so!"

Somehow, I think that Josip will be all right. His mother loves him very much and she is hard at work building a new life for her family in the bombed-out city of Mostar — with her faith to guide her and her parents to help support her.[7]

"As long as we have traveled this far," Patricija said after breakfast the next morning, "you will want to see Split and Dubrovnik. Danijel is getting the car now. If we are lucky, he will agree to stop in Korcula. You have said many times that you want to see our museums. So far, you have seen some in Zadar and Zagreb, but now you will see whole communities that are museums. Then perhaps you will understand something about the people of Croatia. Why we protect our heritage even before we protect our homes."

"This is true," Danijel added. "The Dalmatian coast has always been a center of culture. We are located between Europe and the East along the ancient trade routes. It has been a blessing and a curse. A blessing because trade brings prosperity and culture. A curse because many civilizations sought to control this territory.

"We will go first to Split. You must see Diocletian's Palace."[8] With that, Danijel hit the accelerator and we were off at breakneck speed. "People in the United States read about such things," Danijel said, craning his neck to speak to me in the back seat, "but here we live and breathe history."

When we arrived in Split, we went directly to the palace and the tour began. Danijel wished to climb the bell tower of St. Duje that gives one a marvelous view of the whole palace. However, Patricija and I decided to have coffee in one of the small bistros. While we were sipping our coffee, a man approached me and asked if I would like a guided tour of the palace. I declined, politely, but he would not take no for an answer. Patricija spoke to him also and he became quite agitated. In English, he attacked Patricija's parentage, loyalty and even her religion. Another man, one who knew him, approached and talked him into leaving. Later, our kind rescuer returned and apologized for the man's behavior. "Tomislav is very nervous. Since the war his whole personality has changed. Please believe this is not the behavior of the people in our country."

I assured him that I understood — but it put Patricija in a reflective mood. "Let me explain to you about PTSD (post traumatic stress disorder)," she said. "Do you remember Mario? He was not yet born when the war started, but yet he suffers from it. I will show you when we return to Zadar."

Three days later, back in Zadar, Patricija prepared me to meet Mario by first introducing me to his parents.

" ... *usually when a child draws hearts, the larger the heart,*

the more he is in need of love. ...”

chapter fourteen

Mario's Second-Hand War

Mario is almost six years old. Curly-haired, bright-eyed and curious, he would be a challenge for any parent. For his parents, Andelo and Matea, he is overwhelming. "We have two other children," Matea explained, "and Andelo has problems from the war. He was not wounded in his body, but in his heart. He saw so much!"

"Before the war, Andelo was a carpenter — a very competent carpenter. He also knows much about electricity and plumbing," Matea added. "Since the war, he thinks he is an artist. He got a job once painting scenery for the theater, so now he's an artist," Matea sighed. "Only no one will hire him. There is much work for carpenters, but Andelo does not want to be a carpenter anymore. Most of the time he is at home. He dreams up fantastic machines that no one wants. At night he goes to the cafés to visit with friends. Friends who buy him drinks. Often he is not home until very late. Nonetheless, he is up very early. He does not sleep well. And then there is Mario." Her voice trailed off.

That night I met Andelo. Patricija and Danijel took me to a café along the waterfront and Andelo was there. "He is a good man, but very nervous," Danijel said. "You will see." Andelo talked very quickly, almost staccato. He had brought one of his inventions with him. I talked to him about a problem I was having with deer in my yard, and he flipped over a paper and created a new invention to keep the deer away without hurting them. All the while, he was talking. Sweat glistened on his forehead, although it was not hot. And he chain-smoked. "You want to know about the war? You have no idea. To be in the dark. To know that the enemy is all around. Not to know when he will strike and you will be dead. You cannot run. There are land mines everywhere. No one knows where they are.

You are like a rat in a box. You know someone will kill you soon. The rat does not know that. Then he is there. The man next to you is holding his guts in. *You do not know.*"

He lit another cigarette from the end of the previous one. "Look, what do you think? It is a good invention. No? I will explain it. "

The next morning, I met Mario and his brother and sister. Mario was delightful. His brother and sister said "*Bog,*" and then they were off in the square. Matea called after them to be back by eleven, but they did not hear her. I told Matea that I thought she had a beautiful family. "Beautiful, but willful!" she said. Patricija, Matea, Mario and I walked to a café. I ordered coffee, as did the other women — and produced my ever-ready art supplies. Mario, who already was squirming in his chair, was captivated. I asked him to draw a picture of his Mama and Tata. He was happy to do so … and happy to draw more — a picture of his whole family. Then, because it was something to do, he drew a picture of the flowers they brought to the grave of their grandmother, which is done every year and which is a grand celebration.

When I looked at the picture of his family, I noticed that Tata had no mouth. I asked Mario about this, but all he would say was "Because." His picture of his parents was so unusual … two hearts with eyes but no mouths … walking along hand in hand. I started to say something, but Patricija kicked me under the table, so I complimented Mario on his beautiful flowers.

Later, when we got to Patricija's ambulata, she explained, "Mario drew his father with no mouth because his father shouts at him so much — no mouth, no shouting! And because he threatens to 'cut Mario's eyes out' — no mouth, no threats! No one in the family has arms because every one of them feels helpless. Certainly Mario feels helpless. As for the picture of his parents — usually when a child draws hearts, the larger the heart, the more he is in need of love. It is interesting that the 'heart parents' have no mouths," she said, and dismissed the topic.

"It is very important to understand that there are children who would have had problems whether or not there was a war," she said. "It is a temptation to blame everything on the war. It is sad to say, but this is not always the case. I sometimes think that the problem for most children — certainly the ones I see — is the parent! So I have arranged for you to see and meet children who are not damaged, or perhaps not *too* damaged, by the war.[9] Today you will go to a primary school and meet children who do *not* need to see a psychologist!" With that, she whisked me off to a school near the hospital and left me in the care of several very competent teachers while she returned to the ambulata. Thus, I spent the remainder of the day surrounded by active, laughing, bouncing schoolchildren.

When their teachers told them that I wanted drawings from children, they were only too happy to oblige.

"Drawings of what?" they asked.

"Surprise me," I replied — surprise me they did. They drew pictures of their city, pictures of mermaids and octupi, Christmas and rain showers, basketball and Hale-Bopp — each had a favorite story to share. Some even wrote essays about themselves; *To sam Ja* ("Who Am I?") One young lady, about thirteen, announced that her favorite story was John Grisham's *The Client*. Many of the children wanted to practice their English on me — their fluency was astonishing. Others, of course, were too shy. Some of the children remembered the war, even though they were only two or three years old at the time. Some were evacuated with their families. Others were sent to safety while parents remained in the war zone. They are not unaffected, but they are resilient.

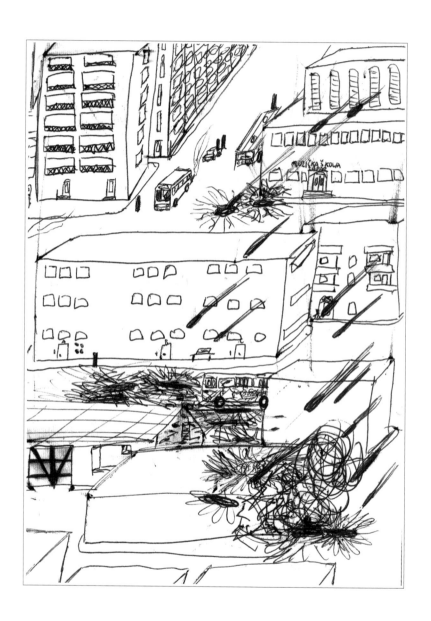

"I was so afraid," she said. "I thought I would die. I mean truly die."

chapter fifteen ✳ Alma, Antonija and Damjan

Alma, Antonija and Damjan are the daughters and son of a family physician and his wife, who is a schoolteacher. During the war, the children remained with their mother and father. Their father was needed to treat the wounded and so Alma, Antonija and Damjan lived in the basement of the hospital with their parents and many other people. During the day, they often spent their time in a pre-school that remained in operation solely to provide care for the children of physicians and nurses who stayed to care for the sick and wounded during the war. This pre-school had a special underground bunker in which the children could be protected during air raids, shelling, and the like. The children's mother taught in the school and Patricija often looked after them when they were "at home" in the hospital's basement because their parents often were busy around the clock, and when they were not busy, they were sleeping. All food and water came from the hospital kitchens, which also were in the basement.

Alma remembers going into the bunker. "The bunker was long, but not very wide. It was damp in there sometimes — we could hear the sounds from outside. It smelled bad, like mildew. Some of the children cried. Sometimes we had to be in there a very long time, but always we got to come out again. One time we were in there so long that Patricija had to bring food to us."

Patricija remembered the incident very clearly. "I was so afraid," she said, "I thought I would die. I mean truly die." The children had been trapped in the bunker for so long that we knew we had to send food. And it was my job to get it there, as everyone else was busy with the wounded. So I took a big tray of sandwiches — the shelling was still going on. The ones I hate the most are the ones that explode above ground, spewing shrapnel everywhere. If you are anywhere around an anti-personnel bomb when it explodes, there will be nothing recognizable left of you. As I said, I was very frightened, like a rabbit. I went as quickly as I could, trying to stay near some protective walls, but in some places there were none. The preschool with the bomb shelter in its front yard stands about 600 meters from the hospital basement — there is a parking lot and a field to cross to get to it. As you can plainly see, both the sandwiches and I arrived safely … but then I had to go back! It is burned into my mind: I had to go back."

Today, these memories are still alive, and so are most of the children. It is important to remember. Most are still alive. And while they have not forgotten, life goes on — and what is happening *now* in a child's life is so much more *immediate*, so much more important. In that immediacy lies the hope of the future. If the air they breathe is clean, freed of adults' hatred and prejudices, there is hope for their future. If the little damaged ones are treated skillfully and nurtured, there is hope for their future. If, as adults, the children embrace the *ideals* of peace and forgiveness and put aside the thirst for justice and vengeance,[10] there is hope for everyone's future.

When the war was going on, all the children wanted was for it to be over. And now it is over and it is time to live again. Even the most well-adjusted children became more aggressive during the war. Now, except for those children suffering from PTSD, it is different. If there is one universal longing among the children, it is still for peace … and a chance to live normally.

The word Sunflower in the Croatian language also means "turning toward the sun." Children instinctively turn toward the light. They are so resilient that even a little bit of light will do. They yearn for it. We adults need only follow them and there will be hope for the world.

Children instinctively turn toward the light…

even a little bit of light will do.

A Note from the Franciscan Sisters of the Poor

In 1995, the Franciscan Health Partnership, Inc. (FRANCISCAN), sponsored by the Franciscan Sisters of the Poor, received a two million dollar grant through the United States Agency for International Development (USAID) – American International Health Alliance (AIHA) to revive, improve and strengthen the health care delivery system serving the communities of Zadar and Biograd in Croatia. The grant called for a three-year action plan for cooperation and exchange of information between the Franciscan hospitals in the United States and the two hospitals in Zadar and Biogard. As part of this partnership, FRANCISCAN has donated over four million dollars in personnel and in-kind support and helped create the Children and Family Society (Foundation).

As part of the FRANCISCAN commitment to the program, the Franciscan Sisters of the Poor Foundation established the Croatian Childrens' Fund to help the children of war-torn Croatia.

Proceeds from the sale of *Sunflowers in the Sand* will benefit the Croatian Childrens' Fund co-chaired by Dr. Zivko Strika and Susan Raymond Ph.D, members of the Board of Governers of the Franciscan Sisters of the Poor Foundation, Inc. Special thanks to the Archbishop of Zadar, Ivan Prenda, Honorary Chairman of the Croatia Children and Family Society, who will be overseeing the use of these funds in Croatia.

Donations to the Croatian Childrens' Fund may be mailed to:
Croatian Childrens' Fund
Franciscan Sisters of the Poor Foundation, Inc.
708 Third Avenue, Suite 200
New York, NY 10017

Footnotes

1. *Bog* is a contraction for "God be with you" and is an informal word for *hello* or *goodbye*.

2. Those who know about such things say that children suffering from post-traumatic stress disorder (PTSD) tend to be more aggressive and spiteful or sometimes more withdrawn and timid. Patricija Padelin indicated that since the war, the incidence of bed-wetting has increased about tenfold.

3. The Croatian government will pay for the rebuilding of the exterior and the interior of the house; it will pay for ten square meters per person living in the house.

4. About 35 percent of the children killed in the war were teenage males.

5. About 500,000 Muslims were "cleansed" in a period of little over six months.

6. Agger, Inger. *Mixed Marriages: Voices from a Psycho-Social held in Zagreb, Croatia.* European Community Humanitarian office, 1995, p. 88

7. Research demonstrates that a child does well if his or her mother adjusts well. See Ajdukovic, Marina and Dean. "Psychological Well-Being of Refugee Children," *Child Abuse & Neglect,* vol. 17, pp. 843–854.

8. Diocletian's Palace is the best-preserved Roman palace extant. Its size is that of a small town.

9. The extent of trauma varies greatly from region to region. One study by school psychologists indicated 9 percent of school children were traumatized and in need of help. Another study showed 56 percent of kindergartners were traumatized and in need of help.

10. Perhaps the only model for this is found in South Africa, where the new government of the majority set up a commission for reconciliation and forgiveness.

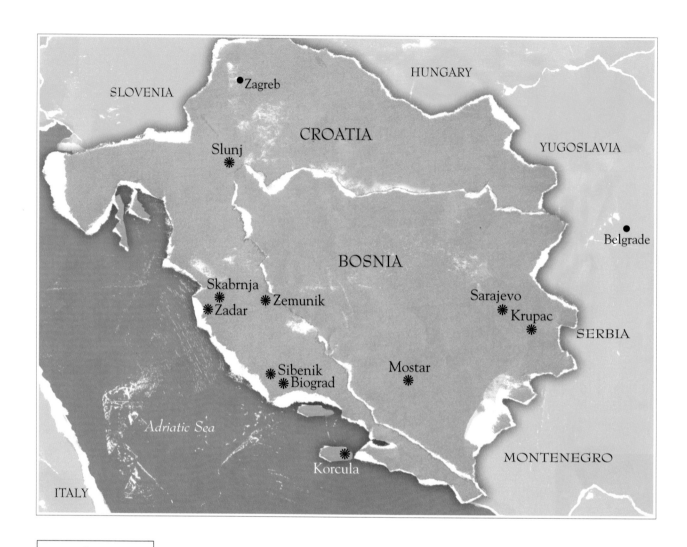

SLOVENIA

HUNGARY

•Zagreb

CROATIA

YUGOSLAVIA

Slunj
✳

•Belgrade

BOSNIA

Skabrnja
✳
✳ Zemunik
✳Zadar

Sarajevo
✳ Krupac
✳

SERBIA

Sibenik
✳
✳ Biograd

Mostar
✳

Adriatic Sea

MONTENEGRO

✳
Korcula

ITALY

50 miles